FOREWORD

The exhibition *Ice and Water* represents a new body of work produced by Peter Fraser during a six week residency in the summer of 1990 in Marseilles. It is the first time this work has been exhibited and constitutes the artist's first solo exhibition in the UK since 1989.

Since the early 1980s Fraser has involved his work exclusively in the development of a particular form of colour image making. It is an area he shares with few other artists. Fraser's focus of attention reminds us of the fragile boundaries between imagination and reality. His confidence in pushing his chosen medium towards certain extremities is further testament of his ability to see the world anew. Fraser's intuitive process reawakes in the viewer a sense of the world as being both chaotic and logical. *Ice and Water* demonstrates his and our suspension of how we view the world when we look at Fraser's work.

The realisation of this project has come about very much because of Peter Fraser's own enthusiasm and energy. It is the result of careful and lengthy preparation and we would like to thank Peter for commitment at all stages. The strength and quality of this work has also been paralleled by Jeremy Millar's challenging text and it is to Jeremy that both Peter and ourselves are especially grateful.

Andrew Cross
James Hockey Gallery

Stephen Snoddy
Cornerhouse

**FRANCIS CLOSE HALL
LEARNING CENTRE**
Swindon Road, Cheltenham
Gloucestershire GL50 4AZ
Telephone: 01242 714600

UNIVERSITY OF
GLOUCESTERSHIRE
at Cheltenham and Gloucester

NORMAL LOAN

655 4/2011

49347 07/06

James Hockey Gallery
WSCAD
FARNHAM

CORNERHOUSE
Manchester

AN UNCERTAIN EXCHANGE

So disfigured was Barthes, as he lay in the road, that no one present recognised him even though the Collège de France was only feet away. He lay for hours at Salpêtrière before being identified.

In his final book, published shortly before his death, Barthes leaves us with a tender expression of his 'realist' position. Against the 'futile' arguments of other commentators, he asserts an existential connection between a photograph and its referent, the overwhelming 'truth' that 'the thing has been there', of a reality that once existed, although it may no longer do so.

It was as he looked amongst the photographs of his recently dead mother that Barthes started on his reflections, driven by a desire to find 'a just image' and not 'just an image' of her, a search for her presence, found, finally, in a photograph of her as a child. It was not Barthes' wish to restore that which has been abolished, to reclaim his mother's body (although he does later link photography to resurrection), but simply to establish her existence, to guarantee her having been. For Barthes, only photography could provide such consolatory proof. To evoke another semiologist, the photograph is seen as indexical, like the death mask.

As he lay in his coffin, a little over a month after his accident, Barthes reconstructed features, were, once more, recognisable.

Although such a tale may seem to tell us very little about Peter Fraser's photographs, it can often be more rewarding to define negatively, an observation taken from the images themselves. For Barthes, the sense of loss was provoked by the slipping of the present into the past, the inexorable slide towards death which the photograph could momentarily halt, but with which it was marked, through and through. There is no such loss in Fraser's photographs, indeed, such loss seems impossible. We may stare, hypnotized, at the oscillation of the floor *Plate 5*, or be held precariously in the wires' grip *Plate 7*, but these are memories of things we have not known, recollections we have not collected. We are drawing on 'a *past* that has never been nor ever will will be present'[1], a past that has not passed. We have entered a new stratification of time.

If these images appear 'dream-like' then perhaps this phenomenon can help us understand this new temporal structure. In dreams, we often know that a protagonist has said something or has acted in a certain way, even though we did not hear the remarks or witness the actions (indeed in dreams we rarely seem to listen to conversations *that* intently, or observe all actions *that* closely, yet this does not seem to diminish our sense of them having happened nor inhibit our attempts at recall). Our memories are no longer dependent on our actions. Our controlling notion of consciousness has finally disintegrated. We have been dislodged from the centre of our own experience.

This sense of perceptual isolation is most visible in *Plate 4*. It is within this image, with its three bands of focus, that the first manifestations of this layering of time can be found, each band corresponding to one of the tenses. The blurred foreground comes to represent the past, the well defined midground, the present, and the indistinct background, the future. In locating the present within the fields of focus, there is a demonstration of our increased awareness of the age in which we find ourselves, a knowledge more acute, *sharper*, than the distortions made of the past or the uncertainties held in the future. Yet doesn't this analysis lie uneasily with the earlier assertion of a *new* stratification of time? Couldn't this be seen as an attempt to restore our central position, both temporally and spatially, like the plastic object? (Norman Mailer says that plastic is the embodiment of Man's vanity — how much greater this is when it comes to represent the vanity of self presence).

Such a desire must go unfulfilled. We must remember our own position in relation to the image, a position which remains external to it. Indeed, if we do inhabit one of its tenses, it must be the past, because it is through the past that we view the image, that we approach the object, that we attempt to claim our place in the present.

Similar movements occur elsewhere. Freud compared our psychic apparatus to the Mystic Writing Pad, a children's toy, still available, which consists of clear acetate sheet covering some greaseproof paper which, in turn, lies upon a waxed base. When a stylus makes contact with the outer layer, this depresses the greaseproof paper which adheres to the wax base, its darkness visible through the lighter upper layers. Any marks made can be removed by simply lifting the paper from the base. Freud had noticed, however, that despite this apparent erasure, the marks remain inscribed upon the wax. This, he proposed, acted similarly to our unconscious, which retains that which it cannot perceive. In turn, the outer sheets became our perception and conscious mind, protecting the unconscious from damage, yet ultimately unable to hold on to that which it impresses upon us.

In his general model of perception and memory, Freud talks of a force moving within the neurological system. As it does so, the force creates a path of lowered electrochemical resistance, a psychological breaching that remains, physically, in the form of an unconscious memory, a trace that will affect future perceptual activity.

Both these ideas are important to Derrida when he comes to expand his concept of writing, relying, as they do, on a casual force which produces a trace, an incision which produces a sign. It is the expression of this mechanical model which becomes primary, the marks it produces on the pad incidental, ultimately, to its working (this is further emphasised when Derrida imagines a perpetual 'erasing' of the perceptual image). Even when the marks *do* appear (and this is the model's importance in relation to this image), they are not the result of the contact between stylus and acetate but of that between the paper and the waxed base. Its appearance comes not from the force pushing down but from the base showing up. To follow the earlier analogy, perception becomes dependent not on the false presence of action, but on the unconscious, on prior breachings, on the *already there*. It is no longer an immediate encounter with the world, but a contact made with that which has been previously inscribed, a coincidence with unconscious memories. We are forever separated, literally, from the presence of the 'the thing itself' (photography's great myth). Of course, this dislocation is also temporal. Unable, as we are, to alter our relation to the image, we are forced to remain in its past. It is a position from which we can never escape, forever barred from the 'now' of our actual experience.

Having followed Derrida this far, perhaps we should continue, passing beyond a materialist concept towards a concept of materialism. If we do so, we find ourselves in an extraordinary position, forced to conceive of matter devoid of reality, a materialism that has been dematerialised. Such positions seems to exist within *Plate 2* and *Plate 5*. These are places which lack definition, which are places between places, placeless places. These are commonplaces and, as we know, it is by now a commonplace that the commonplace is no longer so (it ceases to be so once it begins to signify, and it is its 'truth' that it must signify before it becomes itself). This interchange is invisible. What is pictured here, what can *only* be pictured here, is that which lies simultaneously between them. It does not make visible the invisible — that is absurd — but makes visible 'the extent to which the invisibility of the visible is invisible' [2].

We must begin to realise that emptiness is just as concrete as solid matter. Both are made of weightless, invisible particles, particles which are further surrounded by emptiness. Even our most edifying of structures, our strongest symbols of stability, of origin and elevation, dissolve into a state of *between*. Pillars are slashed by curtains, truncated by shadows. Floors disperse, the tiles transformed into their own particular particles, patterns appearing all the more as the sub-atomic orbits of electrons. A poem about empty space would be sublime. Fraser has photographed it. The focus, like the place, lies elsewhere.

Stranded in this state of dissolution, matter points away from itself, forced to become a signifier before it can become. This is important because it forces us to abandon our conventional method of viewing photographs, as a sign which can be read in reverse. Such a method is evident in Barthes, for instance. If his mother's existence caused an effect photographically, then by looking at the resultant image Barthes hoped to reconstitute the cause, to confirm, if not claim, his mother's presence. The resuscitation of the real is an illusion, however, for how are we to restore that which has never been, a past that has not passed? Instead, deprived of a solid core, we must follow the logic of the exterior, spilling outwards, unfolding endlessly. This further emphasises the eccentricity of the positions in which we have found ourselves. Just as our memories (and indeed our perceptions) appear unrelated to our actual experiences, so too do the meanings brought forth by these photographs. Signifying occurs outside of the self, a movement of meaning from which we are excluded, an opening up beyond ourselves, ungraspable and out of reach.

In surrendering ourself, we are finally approaching a state of meditation. We must concentrate as the photographs do, on the rocks, the plastic object, the edge of the water, not so that they intensify and become rooted, but instead disperse, move out from themselves. This dissemination must proceed unhindered, free to unfold and expand, to move without containment. We must therefore create a sense of emptiness, a sense of void, a limitless space which opens up on all sides. It is within this absence, this negativity, that meaning is created, expanding invisibly, quietly, infinitely.

Marco Polo describes a bridge, stone by stone.
'But which is the stone that supports the bridge?' Kublai Khan asks.
'The bridge is not supported by one stone or another', Marco answers, 'but by the line of the arch that they form'.
Kublai Khan remains silent, reflecting. Then he adds: 'Why do you speak to me of the stones? It is only the arch that matters to me'.
Polo answers: 'Without stones there is no arch'[3].

How would Marco Polo describe Fraser's work? He would, without doubt, be wise to the quiet interpretations that lived within his words, aware of the inability to describe things as they are (as what they are depends on how they are described). He would, almost certainly, be conscious of his judgement as one amongst many, whose elements can be rearranged, subject to a different sort of selection, a different method of support. He would presumably say that, like the stones which make up the bridge, no single idea holds together the interpretation in which it is found, wary that the structure which he builds may disguise the parts from which it is made. We would do well to remember these things. Like Marco Polo, we too must strive for a sense of coexistence, careful that the construction of one way of looking does not simply become the destruction of others.

This sense of simultaneity occurs in *Plate 1*. Here, too, we find rocks, chipped and flat on a smooth, scarred surface. The light, a cold, chemical radiation, emphasizes the uncertainty, a scene vaguely distinct. Movements have marked the floor as traces of intrusion, yet these are slight impressions. Ultimately, it is the sense of abandonment which overwhelms. This is the result of invisibility rather than absence. Forces always exist, even if only potentially, yet those here make no attempt to neutralize their opposite.

Photography has surveyed this state before. In 1920, Marcel Duchamp left his studio and, with Man Ray, went to dinner. In the studio, Man Ray had left his camera slowly collecting an image of the dust which Duchamp's *Large Glass* was, itself, slowly collecting.

What is perhaps the most interesting aspect of *Dust Breeding*, the resultant print, is not the conceptual and physical symmetry of its production but the forms which the particles have begun to take (like clouds, thickening and dissolving, hiding and revealing the roads which define, and are defined by, the fields which surround them). While the dust could be seen as the gradual disintegration of the original object, their consolidation seems to run contrary to this process of entropic disposal. This is undoubtedly no synthesis, but it is not an attempt to isolate effects either. Instead, both images become sites of an undecidable exchange, within themselves and between each other.

If binary oppositions are to be found within Fraser's photographs, it is only that these distinctions be dismantled. This is undoubtedly true of those present in *Plate 7*. An interior wall slips into the distance, its harsh surface dissolving as it does so. The light, once more, seems visible, a thickening emergence from its two sources. A wire enters the frame, blue like the daylight which lines that edge. Another curves to penetrate the artificial warmth in the centre, as though its colour supplies, or is supplied by it. The smaller wires appear from the holes opposite their larger relations, their oscillations held by the line of focus.

Denied the terminus of meaning (and hence a unifying position), matter is transferred within this area of exchange. It is here that the wall begins to melt, as though fused by its own dynamics. The heat contained within the scene begins to flow spontaneously, in an attempt to disperse evenly, that their randomness might end in rest. Yet this movement towards thermal equilibrium proves impossible, obstructed by its own incessant circularity. As the energy is conducted, from the centre, we realise that this warmth is indeed artificial, the consequence of emotional calorescence rather than any actual physical attribute. The real exchange, the actual transference of energy, occurs in the opposite direction, from the blue heat to the red cool, from the hot edges to the cold heart[4].

It is an image of incredible unrest, literally, elements oscillating, uncertain of their own attributes, colour temperatures undermining their chromatic expression. It lies along the edge of the undecidable, questioning the rationality of photographic realism as opposed to irrational artistic expression, questions which are contained within, and which contain, all these photographs.

For all the uncertainty which surrounds these photographs, there are elements of crystallisation, at which order begins to form. However, this has little to do with rigidity, its state, in many ways, as precarious and shifting as the inconsistencies which it would appear to dispel. It is, in effect, not a state at all, but a stage, the entering of the photographs, and the spaces between them, into 'phase transition'.

While we may find such a position difficult to conceive of, it is not an unusual situation, perhaps the simplest example given of this being the melting of an icecube. Within the ice, its molecules are locked into a rigid crystalline structure, an ordered condition; with the fluidity of water, its ease of movement represents a state of inconstancy. But there is between, a stage where the ice is just melting, water lying on its surface, ice floating in the river which surrounds its main form. This is the phase transition between ice and water, solid and liquid, the area of exchange between two seemingly separate elements. We are travelling along the edge of chaos.

Although the water held in *Plate 9* would appear to have come to rest, its stability is in many ways the consequence of constant activity. But this is a movement to deny movement, an agitation, a molecular binding, which tightens form and eliminates excess areas. The water, like the series itself, has a surface tension, a need to restrain. This is not to deny possibilities, however, but to increase potential, to force a more meaningful breaching (like that which passes between the wires). As a liquid it becomes almost solid, a reclaiming of the structure which it had been denied, but only that this may dismantle more completely such restraint (it has been said that every system contains the makings of its own destruction).

We must therefore begin to recognise not only the possibilities of *difference* but also the different as *possible*, not simply to be identified but also identified *with*. We can no longer say that opposites attract because there are no longer any opposites. Even when energy travels between points, between wires, it does not take the form of a simple exchange:

'Rather their relationship takes the form of a spiral which no simple infraction can exhaust. Perhaps it is like a flash of lightning in the night which, from the beginning of time, gives a dense and black intensity to the night which it denies, which lights up the night from the inside, from top to bottom, and yet owes to the dark the stark clarity of its manifestation, its harrowing and poised singularity'[5].

Difference is no longer a position we must oppose, but one which we cannot help adopt. The effect is disorientating, a dizzying reversal where what once undermined now helps to define, a dissolving of independence to the point where support becomes a play of relations.

For all the structure of its geometric forms, *Plate 6* shares this sense of uneasy stability. The metal spikes are thrust aggressively towards the concrete form, the anticipated points of contact already marked as if in preparation, resigned to the inevitability of their destruction. Yet for all its supposed menace, the one encounter is almost gentle. The concrete seems to envelope the spike, forming a halo around its tip as if to emphasize and embrace. It remains the only visible means of support for the concrete, yet one which remains a caress however uncertain. This is an image which contains an unexpected tenderness (in that the tender embraces both the soft and the sore), which carries within it both pleasure and pain, indeed a pleasure derived from pain, a sentiment of the sublime. It is from this equivocal emotion that the image acquires its unmistakable eroticism, more visceral than visual. We are left with a terrible beauty, intimate and enigmatic, like waking with a bruise one didn't have before.

Jeremy Millar

NOTES

1. Jacques Derrida, 'Différence', *Speech and Phenomena, and Other Essays on Husserl's Theory of Signs*, Northwestern University Press, Ill. 1973, p. 152.
2. Michel Foucault, 'Maurice Blanchot: The Thought from Outside', *Foucault-Blanchot*, Zone Books, New York. 1990, p. 24.
3. Italo Calvino, *Invisible Cities*, Secker & Warburg, London. 1974, p. 82.
4. Although it may appear contrary to our usual perceptions, blue daylight has a considerably higher colour temperature than the comforting effects of glowing tungsten.
5. Michel Foucault, 'Preface to Transgression', *Language, Counter-Memory, Practice*, edited by Donald F. Bouchard, Cornell University Press, Ithaca, N.Y. 1977, p. 35.

Plate 1

Plate 2

Plate 3

Plate 4

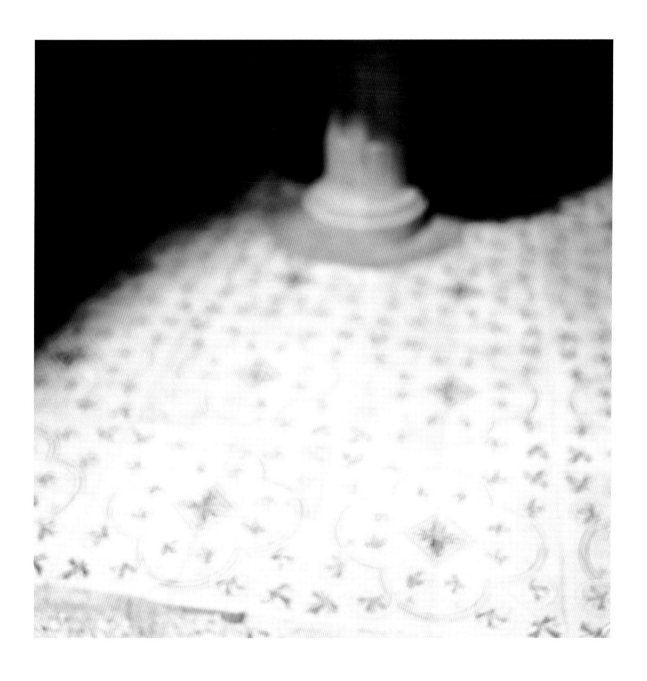

Plate 5

Plate 6

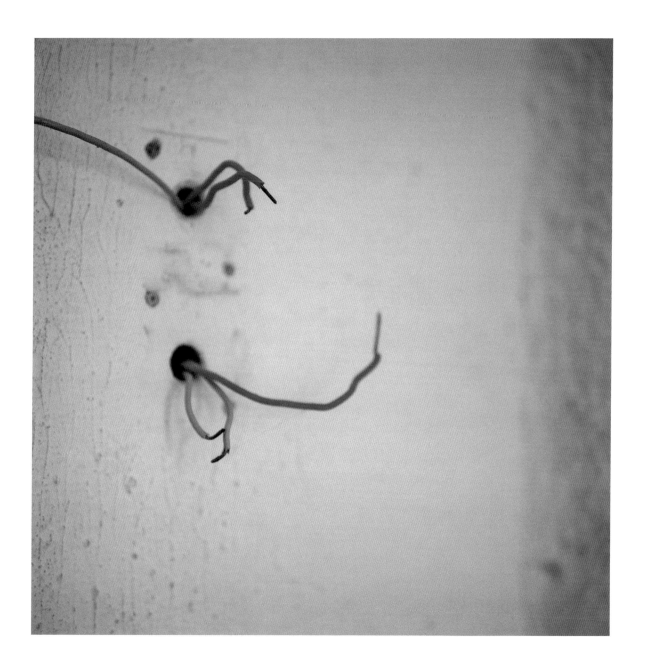

Plate 7

Plate 8

Plate 9

Plate 10

Peter Fraser

Peter Fraser was born in Cardiff, Wales in
1953. He studied Photography at
Manchester Polytechnic and after living in
Bristol for a number of years he presently
lives and works in London.

Since his first solo exhibition at Impressions
Gallery, York in 1982 Fraser has exhibited
internationally in a number of solo and group
exhibitions.

In 1988 a monograph of Fraser's work,
entitled *Two Blue Buckets* was published by
Cornerhouse Publications. His work is
represented in a number of private and public
collections in the UK and abroad.

All photographs in the exhibition measure
1.25m square.

Ice and Water

Published in an edition of 500 to coincide
with the exhibition at

Cornerhouse   19 March − 24 April 1993
James Hockey Gallery   July/September 1993

Text © Jeremy Millar, Cornerhouse and
James Hockey Gallery March 1993
ISBN 1 897586 05 1

Originated and printed by
Offset Colour Print
Southampton
Telephone + 44 (0) 703 632111

James Hockey Gallery
West Surrey College of Art & Design
Farnham
Surrey GU9 7DS
Telephone + 44 (0) 252 732241
Facsimile + 44 (0) 252 733869

Cornerhouse
70 Oxford Street
Manchester M1 5NH
Telephone + 44 (0) 61 228 7621
Facsimile + 44 (0) 61 236 7323

James Hockey Gallery gratefully
acknowledges financial assistance from
South East Arts Board.

Cornerhouse gratefully acknowledges
financial support from North West Arts Board,
British Film Institute, Association of Greater
Manchester Authorities and the
Henry Moore Foundation.

For this exhibition the organisers would
like to thank the Office de la Culture,
Ville de Marseilles.